I0697399

Table of Contents

Introduction

Investing your money is one of the best ways to ensure that your money will go to work and start growing, without you needing to come up with a second or a third job. There are many different forms of investing that an investor can choose, based on what they like to do and the level of risk that they would like to take on. Some will dive into the stock market while others may try starting their own business. One option that you can consider is residential real estate.

Residential real estate involves any work that is done in residential properties. These are generally properties under five units where people will make their home. They can include single-family homes, duplexes, and more and you can choose whether to purchase the property and flip it or to rent it out to tenants and make an income in that manner. While there are a lot of components that need to come together to start in residential real estate, it can prove to be a lucrative investment.

This guidebook is going to dive more into the world of real estate investing. We will look more at what is considered residential property and some of the strategies that you can use to help get started in this investment. The type that you choose will depend on your overall goals and what you hope to accomplish. For example, you could fix and flip a property or purchase a multi-unit property and live in part of the home while renting out the rest.

Once you have your strategy in place, it is time to get to work, knowing what to look for when you want to purchase a residential property. You will need to consider the price of the property, the work that needs to be done, and even whether the price is right for what you want to do. Part of this process includes a property valuation and a look at financing the investment to make sure that you are prepared to take on all the work for this investment.

One component that a lot of investors forget about when investing is the tax implications. This can quickly turn into a business, rather than just buying and selling properties as an individual and this guidebook will talk about when this happens and what you can do to handle some of the tax implications that come from this kind of business. Many components come with starting your investment in residential real estate. To finish things off, we will look at whether you need to work with a property manager, whether you should use a contractor to fix up the property or do it yourself, and some of the barriers and fears that can get in the way. As that comes together, you will be able to grow your real estate empire and turn this into a truly amazing form of investing your money.

While there are a lot of different types of investing that you can choose to do, not all of them are going to work out well and may have a good deal of risk. When you choose to work with residential real estate, you have the power to control the investment, choosing how long to keep the property, whether to rent it out or not and so much more. Let's take a look through this guidebook to learn as much as possible about residential real estate investing and why it may be the right option for you.

Chapter 1: What is Considered a Residential Property

There are a lot of different types of investing that you can choose to work with. When you take your time to research real estate, it can be a lucrative way to make some money. Most real estate investors will need to choose between residential and commercial real estate, with many choosing to go with residential real estate because it is less costly (in most cases) and has a larger audience than a commercial property will be.

If you are looking to purchase and sell residential property, it is you need to spend time looking at the different properties and see which ones will fit into the category of real estate for residential property. to keep it simply a residential property is going to be a type of real estate that has been zoned or developed for living, rather than for a business. This will include a large number of buildings for you to choose.

Any property that is available for occupation for any non-business purpose, so anything that people can live in, will be a residential property. These can be attractive to many tenants or buyers who are ready to find the perfect home, making it a lucrative investment source if you are willing to look around and research and find the right one. Some of the most common types of residential properties that you can choose include:

1. Condominiums; These are going to be privately owned units that are within a large building or some kind of communities. They work similar to an apartment, but they will be owned by the person who lives in the unit.
2. Townhomes: These are units that are going to be a big bigger than the condo and will have fewer of them together. It will usually share its walls with one or two other buildings depending on the size of it.
3. Cooperatives: These are going to be units that are inside one building where everyone who is inside of the building will own that together.
4. Single-family houses: These are going to be a common type of property that you want to use for families and when you would like to sell the property rather than renting it out. It will have a single lot and will not have any space that it needs to share with another dwelling.
5. Multi-family homes: These are going to have less than an apartment, but will still have a few together. A four-plex or a duplex with two to four units are common for these. In most cases, anything larger than the four units will be. A commercial property instead.

In most definitions of residential properties, apartments are not going to count unless they have four or fewer units in them. They are often considered more of a commercial property so will not be brought up in the process here. In addition, temporary living spots, campgrounds, and hotels are not going to be included in this type of property either.

What is the Difference Between Residential and Commercial Property?

When you are going to invest in real estate that is residential, it is a good idea to look at how this type of investment is going to be different than commercial properties. Commercial real estate is going to be different than residential because it is more business-focused instead of one where people will live inside of the property. The residential property will have individuals who will move in and make it their home while the commercial property is going to be designed for a business to do their work in.

If you want to have a property that someone is going to either purchase and lease from you to run their business, then you would want to go with the commercial property to make your money. However, if you are looking to work with a families or individuals, selling them a great home or being a landlord as they rent their home from you, then residential properties are right for you.

Benefits of Investing in Residential Real Estate

All types of investments are going to carry some risks, but investing in real estate is a great way to put your money to work and earn a good profit when it is done the right way. There are a number of benefits to choosing to invest in residential real estate including:

Long Term Investment

Investing in residential property is going to be a long-lasting investment. This is an investing that has a lot of security when it comes to your money. As long as you are careful, you will be able to earn money off the property, which may be harder to do with some of the other investments you choose. You will either need to get a good deal and move quickly if you are flipping a home, or hold onto the home for a while to see the value grow.

Residential real estate is also going to offer the value of appreciation as time goes by. The more time that passes, the more value you will have out of the property as well. This is known as capital appreciation and is going to be a good way for you to enjoy profits from your hard work.

Absolute Ownership

Unlike what you will see with commercial properties and apartments, the residential investment is going to allow the investor to have absolute ownership. You will have complete freedom to revamp the property as you would like, on how to use the property, and how long you would like to own the property too.

As the boss, you will be able to do what you would like with the property. You can choose to sell it, rent it out, or renovate it to the way that you would like. If you purchase a commercial property, you will not be able to do what you want with the property. You can renovate it to make it more usable, but you have to think about the final customer and how they would use the property before you do anything with it.

Exemption from Tax

There are some different tax benefits to running your residential real estate business. You will need to hire a professional CPA to help with all of this, but you can utilize the proceeds in the right way to make more money and to keep your taxes at a minimum, making this a good way to invest in yourself.

Steady Cash Flow from the Property

There are several ways that you can make cash flow from your residential property, especially if you are ready to rent it out to others and earn money that way. Many will choose to purchase the property, fix it up a little bit, and then rent it out to others as an investment as well. They can get the cash flow from the rents each month and still own the property. This will help them to get the appreciation on the property too, which they can use later on to help them if they wish to sell and earn that money as well.

This kind of cash flow is hard to get with other forms of investments. You will either need to sell the investment overall or do something else with it to make sure that you get the results that you want. But it is possible with a residential property, which can make it really appealing to a lot of people.

There are so many things that you are able to do with a residential property when you decide to use this as your form of investing. It is relative safe and secure, can provide cash flow, and lets you be in charge of what you do with the property from the very beginning. This makes it much better type of investment than you can see compared to some of the other choices out there.

Chapter 2: Real Estate Investment Strategies

There are a number of different strategies that you can choose when you want to invest in real estate. Some of the strategies will work well if you have a commercial property and others are best for the residential properties that we will discuss in this guidebook. Learning the basics of each one will make it easier for you to understand how real estate investing works and provides you with some idea of how you would like to get started for the best results. Some of the different residential real estate investment strategies that you can choose include:

Buy and Holds

One investment strategy to try is a buy and hold. These are going to be good as a long-term investment in real estate because they provide a steady additional income and the opportunity for the investor to gain appreciation. If you are looking for an active and long-term investment, then the buy and hold is the best way to go.

Buying an investment property this way requires that the investor will do some research about the market, the area the home is in, and the expenses of this property. the investor needs to make sure they will get a positive cash flow or they will lose money each month. With the buy an hold, deciding to become a landlord, or working with a property manager can be something important here too.

Keep in mind that not all of the buy and hold properties are going to be the same. You can choose to go with a single family home or a duplex. Depending on the cash flow and the location of the property, an investor might choose to rent out individual rooms in the property or the entire home.

For investing this way, a multi-family home is popular. They are able to split up the home between more than one tenant and many will choose to live in one of the parts. They will get some income plus their own rent taken care of at the same time. There are many options here, but the investor is often able to make money from rents during their ownership and from appreciation on the property.

No matter the type of buy and hold property, you will need to get the property and get it fixed up as soon as possible. Start listing that the area is for rent before long so that you can vet and get the tenants in there before you have the property. The more that you can have a tenant pay for the mortgage, the more money that you can earn from this type of investment.

REIT

Investors can also choose to invest in a REIT, or a real estate investment trust. This is going to be a company that owns, operates and finances income-generating real estate. It is similar to a mutual fund because the REIT will pool in the capital from many investors all at once. This makes it possible for investors to earn dividends from investing in real estate, without the hassle of having to purchase, manage, and finance the property on their own.

The properties that fit into the REIT may include data centers, healthcare facilities, apartment complexes, hotels, and more. You can specifically choose to go with an REIT that is for just residential properties or go with something that is going to be for other buildings as well. Most of the REITs that you choose are going to specialize in a specific sector of real estate. However, diversified and specialty REITs can hold onto a lot of different property types in the same portfolio.

There are several types of REITs that you can choose to invest in. some of the most common types include:

1. Equity REITs: Most of the REITs that you choose will be equity REITs. These will own and manage real estate that will produce income. Revenues are often going to be generated through the rent, rather than reselling the property.

2. Mortgage REITs: These will often lend money to real estate owners and operators through loans or mortgages or through the acquisition of mortgage-backed securities. The earnings that come form this are often from the net interest margin, which is just the spread between the interest they can earn on the loans and the cost for funding these loans. This model will make them sensitive to increases in interest rates.

3. Hybrid REITs: These are going to be special types of REITs that will use both the mortgage and the equity REIT from above.

These generally have less risk because they allow the investor to put money into a pool with a lot of other investors and then earning money. The return on investment can be lower, but it is a good place to start when you want to invest in the real estate market.

BRRR Investing

Another type of investment to try is the BRRRR investing option. This stands for Buy, Rehab, Rent, Refinance, Repeat. This can help you to really get a lot of properties going while earning money in the process. If it is done well, it is bale to provide a passive income as well as a revolving method for purchasing and owning rental property. The exact steps that you would follow for this method includes:

1. Buy a property: You need to go for a distressed property that will need some work to get it to code and ready for a rental. Because of the condition of the property, it is less expensive to purchase.
2. Rehab the property: When you have purchased the property, you will need to do all of the rehab. This can take some time because of the original condition of the property. Get it prepared for renters.
3. Rent out the property: When the home is rehabbed, it is time to find the rental price and find tenants to fill it.
4. Refinance: You will need to do a cash-out refinance at this point. This allow you to convert the equity that you have in the property into cash. You can take out a bigger mortgage and then keep the cash to use to another property.
5. Repeat: Use the money from the refinance to get another property and then repeat the process until you build up your empire.

This one is going to take some work to get done, and you need to work fast, be good at keeping costs down, and have a good credit score, but it can be a great way to make money in real estate.

Syndication

A real estate syndication is going to be when income property investors will come together to help finance a property investment. There can be a few investors involved in this or there can be hundreds. These investors are going to work to pool together all of their financial resources to start the investment and they can also share any of the other real estate investing resources that are available.

This works because it allows the income property investors to make a profit and further their careers in real estate at a much larger scale than they would be able to do with some of their own finances at the time. The more people to invest together in the syndication, the more successful it will be.

There are two basic roles that are found in a syndication. This includes the sponsor and the rest of the investors. The sponsor is going to be crucial to these investment properties. The investors will rely on the knowledge of the sponsor to help them:

1. Find the right properties to invest in.
2. Get sufficient financing for all rental properties.
3. Acquire the property that they are investing in.
4. Be responsible for some of the daily tasks for the rental property management.

Besides investing time into the property, the sponsor is also going to invest some of their own financial equity as well. This can be somewhere between five to twenty percent of the total equity capital for the real estate investment.

Then there are also the real estate investors. These investors will often just invest money, putting in 80 to 95% of the total equity capital for the investment. Since they are not going to invest the sweat equity, this can become a passive form of investing.

Airbnb Investment Properties

Some investors are going to take some time to work in residential real estate and have Airbnb's. these are a type of buy and hold property that is going to work more as a short-term or vacation rental. You will need to look at these a little differently than you do for some of the other choices. For example, how will you handle the frequent turnovers with the tenants? How are vacation occupancy rates in your area? Are there legal things to consider with this type of investment?

There are many investors who are looking to get into the business of Airbnb because it can be lucrative, if it is done the right way. You need to be really careful about this and pick the right property. just because rentals are popular in an area does not mean you can find an affordable place to purchase to join in. Many of the investors who are doing this now got the property years ago when prices were cheaper.

Fix and Flips

If the long-term option is not something that appeals to you, it is time to look for something that is more short-term and will provide you with a good cash flow too. As long as you do this well, you can purchase and then sell the property quickly and keep the profits. Basically, the fix and flips will include some properties that the investors buys, renovates, and then sells for more money later on.

This is not a get rick quick scheme, like some of the shows on TV like to portray them. You have to find a good deal, know how to make the fixes quickly, and get it back on the market as well. You should always have a list of deal breakers when coming up with the property. For example, how much are you willing to spend on the property and what are some types of fixes you know are too expensive and you will not waste your time on. Take your time with this to make sure that you get the right property and do not lose money.

Time is not going to be your friend when it comes to a fix or flip property. The faster that you are able to get the work done, the more money you could potentially make. Once you put in the offer on the home, you need to have the materials on stand-by and the contractors ready to go. This will help you get into the home on the first day.

If you keep the home on the market for a year or more, you will have to pay all the taxes, the insurance, and the mortgage payments from one month to the next. This is going to cut into the final amount that you are able to get when you sell the home. If you can get the work done in just a few weeks and put the home back on the market, then you will only have to pay one or two months of mortgage before making your money.

Passive Investments

For investors who want to get into residential real estate but do not want to get their hands dirty, or who do not have the time to do the work themselves, then doing a passive investment is going to be one of the best options. There are a few methods to work with for this. For example, the Real Estate Investment Trust, or REIT, is where a group of investors are going to pool together their money in order to purchase a lot of singe-family home or even some commercial properties.

Each investor, if it goes well, get to share in the profits after it is done, but they do not have all the risk since a lot of them will work together rather than one person putting in all of the money. The return on investment is often lower on this kind of choice, but it is going to also reduce the amount of risk that you have too.

Another option if you would like to passively invest in real estate is to lend money to any investor who would like to flip their own property. Some investors are going to have trouble getting a traditional loan through the bank, especially if they want to get a property that needs work and is vacant. You can provide them with some of the funding and then receive the interest payments on the loan and the final payment when the term of the loan is done. The property is your security for the loan.

Real Estate Wholesaling

It is possible to make some good money in real estate, without having to spend a lot of your own money either. And with all of the great opportunities out there to invest, you will be able to find the right method for you. one of the options that you can choose is wholesaling.

Wholesaling is a great way to create an income without having to really spend money. The wholesaler is going to find a seller who wants to put a residential property up for sale, but that property has not made it on the market yet. The wholesaler is then going to find the right buyer for the property and will get a share of the selling price. You have to have a good network and a database of potential buyers and sellers for the best results.

Residential real estate investors will have a lot of choices they can make to help them to earn money and have a lot of fun in the process. It will take time, research, and a good eye for the market. But with so many different strategies available, the investor will be able to find the right method for them.

Chapter 3: What to Look for When Purchasing a Residential Property

Once you have decided that it is time to go into residential real estate, you will need to go shopping for a property. You have probably already had your eye on a few different properties, and now it is time to get to work looking at all of the different types of properties that have the potential for becoming your investment.

Not all properties that come on the market will work for you. there are many great properties, but you need one that is affordable, will be undervalued, and does not need a lot of work. Some of the things that you should take a look at when purchasing a residential property for your investment include:

Whether It Will Work as a Rental or a Flip

When looking through some of the properties that you would like to invest in, you must consider whether you would like to work with a rental property or one that you would like to flip. The way that you plan to work with the home will determine whether a particular property is going to work for your investment.

Have this in mind from the start. This will make it easier for you to look for the right type of properties. It can limit the area you shop in, the price that you go with, and other factors of your investment.

The Current Cost of the Home

You have to take a look at the current cost of the home before you make a purchase. If the home is already priced at or really close to market value, even if it needs a lot of renovations and fixes, then this is not a good investment for you. When the home is listed for a decent price and you feel that a few updates would make it worth a lot more, you may find that this is a good property to invest in.

The Cost for Renovations

For those who want to get into residential real estate and would like to flip the property, it is time to look at the costs of the renovations. To get a good deal on a property, you will likely need to put in some work to get the home looking nice. Some of the renovations will be as simple as fixing a few things and adding in a fresh coat of paint, and others may require professionals to come in.

As you look at the home, you will need to look at the estimated costs for getting work done. The more you do this type of investing, the better you will get at estimating while looking at the home. If you are uncertain about a price, go look it up or call a contractor to get a better idea. Add up the total of the renovations and the cost of the home. Subtract that from what you think you could sell the home for. If there is no profit found there, or the profit is too low, then it is best to go with a different property.

The Price of Rentals

For a residential real estate investor who is looking to turn the property into a rental, they need to look carefully at the prices of rents in that area. If it is a big city, be aware that different parts of the city will provide different rental prices. The size of the building (such as being a three or four bedroom), the amenities in the property (such as having a pool), and whether it is a single-family home or a duplex will factor in to the rental price.

When looking at a property, you will need to have a good idea how much you would be able to get out of it for rent. This is a number that will guide your decisions. Once you factor in closing costs, renovations, payments on the property while you get it ready, and then time to find a tenant, along with taxes and insurance, will the price you can get for renting it out be enough? That answer will tell you whether this is a good property to invest in.

What Amenities are Nearby

The closer the property is to a wide variety of different amenities, the easier it will be for you to find a tenant or a good buyer in the future. People want to live where there are things to do. If you purchase a property that is near the downtown area, close to businesses and the restaurants, then you have a great place for young adults or business people to call home in that property.

If you would like to attract families to the property, then searching for a property that is near to the schools, close to parks, and other amenities like the library, museums, and other forms of entertainment can be a great option.

Elderly tenants and buyers will be a little different. While some like to be close to families and may hold onto their old homes for years for that very purpose, it is also common that when someone from this age group does look to purchase a new home, they like to be around others who are similar in age, and in more of a quiet community. You will want to look for a home that meets these requirements.

What are the Features of the Property?

This requires that the investor takes some time to look the property over. You need to get in the mind of your tenant or a potential seller and see what they would like about the property, or what you could add to the property when preparing it for selling, without spending a lot of money.

Does the home have three or four bedrooms and a few bathrooms? These are popular for families so they have enough room for their kids. Is the yard big or smaller? A small yard may be good for an elderly buyer or tenant who does not want a lot of yard upkeep but a bigger one is good for those who want some space. Are there interesting features, like a fireplace, that you could enhance and bring to life with a little work?

Take a good look around any property that you would like to purchase and see what some of the features are. Even if it is worn down and falling apart, there is bound to be a few good things that are inside that you can liven up and make look better. Focusing on those can help you find some good treasures that may go unnoticed and can snag them for a good deal.

Are There Any Concerns in the Area?

It is a good idea to look not just at the property, but also at some of the neighborhood that is around the property. if there are some major concerns with the neighborhood, then it may not be a good idea to fix up the home and rent or sell it.

When you rent out a single-family home, or even sell it, you are most likely going to have a lot of families who will want to move into the property. They want to have a safe spot for their kids to live in, a safe spot to walk around, ride bikes, and have fun. It does not matter how much you dress up a home, if it is in a bad area, it is going to struggle to get tenants or a buyer to even look at it.

However, if you are able to find a run down home that is in a great neighborhood, next to good schools and jobs and parks, then you are in luck. Sometimes good homes are passed up on because of their appearances. A little bit of work can instantly increase the value and make this worth more than before. You can swoop in and get the home for an affordable price if you are willing to wait and be patient, and then get it ready to make money.

How Is the Current Market?

You can spend all day looking at properties and hoping that you find a good one, but it is hard to know whether you are getting a good deal on the property or not if you do not look at the market where the home is currently located in.

You do not want to look at the full market in the whole country. It is possible for individual markets to be completely different than what the overall market is doing in a whole country. Purchasing a home just because the market is hot in a few places is a bad idea. That area may have good deals on homes because no one wants to live there and the market has crashed, making it hard for you to earn money.

In some areas, you may be able to find a hot market, even if most of the country is dealing with a lower trend. This is a good place to invest in because some buyers are not going to be ready to jump in yet. You need to know the market before you make any purchase.

Always do a market analysis of the property before you make a purchase. This will help you get a better idea on how much you will be able to make off the property when it is time to sell it. If the market does not look good in that area, you can run the numbers to see if it is still worth it. Never jump in with any home purchase or you will end up wasting money.

As a residential real estate investor, you need to take your time to look at a home thoroughly and see if it is worth your money to invest in. This is true whether you are looking for a rental property or you would like to fix up the property and flip it. By looking at some of the factors above, you can pick a property that is going to suit all of your needs.

Chapter 4: Property Valuation

All investors will need to do a property valuation in order to make the best decisions on their investments. Not every property, whether you plan to flip it or use it as a rental income, is going to provide you with the same yield. At first glance, it may seem that two properties are equal, but you need to dive down into things a little bit more to figure out the true numbers of the investment.

When the investor is able to accurately value the property, they will be able to scale up their portfolio and avoid buying something that is going to be a big mistake. Let's take a closer look at property valuation and the steps that you can take to make this successful.

What is Property Valuation?

The first step is to understand what a property valuation is all about. A property valuation is going to be the calculations that investors in real estate will use to figure out what the value of the property is. Property valuations can be done by investors who use specific data on the market and the property. it is also often done by a licensed appraiser and by real estate brokers to find out the value of that property.

Before you start to figure out what the value of a property is, you will need to collect some key financial data for the property. Some of the numbers that you need to do this include:

1. Mortgage payment: You need to also know whether this payment includes insurance and property taxes too.
2. The down payment about. This is going to vary based on what mortgage the investor gets and the type of investment strategy they will use.
3. Rental income: This needs to include the allowance for a vacancy and how much cash flow there will be after the investor pays for the mortgage and their normal operating expenses.
4. Renovation costs. If the investor wants to flip the home, they will need to figure out the costs to fix up the property and how long they will need to make payments before putting it back on the market.
5. Price to income ratio. This is going to compare the median home price to the median income in the market. As the ratio decreases, the homes will become more affordable to purchase. This can make it easier to flip and easier to find the right tenants for a rental property too.
6. Gross rental yield; This is a number that we can find by dividing the total purchase price of the home, which needs to include the closing costs and fees along with all improvements that you need to make, by the annual gross

rent. The higher the rental yield percentage, the better the property is for your investment.

7. Capitalization rate: This is going to be the rate of return that the investor can get on the rental property. This is found by dividing the net operating income by the market value of the home. This is not going to compare how much the financing will cost, which makes it easier to do a comparison of all similar properties in that area.

8. Cash flow: This is going to be the money that is left over after all of the expenses for the property. This can be measured on an annual or a monthly basis. Negative cash flow can sometimes occur do, which means that the amount to handle the property is more than the rental income that you get.

What Factors Affect the Value of the Property?

There are several factors that you need to consider to determine if a property is going to be a good value for you or not. Some of the things to consider includes:

The Size of the Property and the Floor Plan

The price per square foot is a good metric to use when valuing the residential property. this is because, even though you may look at the ROI and cap rate to help see how much income the property is going to use, the exit strategy may call on you to sell the property to another owner who may not be an investor.

In addition to looking that the square footage, you need to consider the floor plan of the property, including the bathrooms and bedrooms. Just because you have found a bigger home does not mean that it is a better value for you. the characteristics of the home need to meet with your target renter and the market. For example, a home with three bedrooms and one bathroom may not work well for an investment because people want two bathrooms. Even one-bedroom homes in a college town may not work because more students want to have roommates to share the rent.

Improvements to the Property

Some single-family rentals where the owner of the property have made improvements can be a great deal. That is because you will not need to do a lot of improvements in order to raise the value of the property. Some improvements do not provide the return on investment that you want. If the seller does some of the work for you, you will be able to get the benefits later, without all of the costs.

Condition of the Property

As an investor, you will need to take a good look at the property. The more work that you need to do to a home, the more it is going to cost you and the less in profits you will be able to make on the home. Deferred maintenance items, like a heating system or a roof that needs to be replaced or a floor plan that is bad can reduce the value of the property because you will need to spend more money to update it.

Age of Property

It is common that a new property is going to have a higher value compared to older ones. This is because there are fewer routine repairs and fewer capital improvements that the homeowner would need to take care of in the foreseeable future. This can make it a better value if you can get it for a good price.

The Location

You should consider the location of the property. this is going to affect things like whether people want to live in that area, the growth for jobs in the market, the tax rates, and more. You need to shop around to find the right location to help you to choose the right property so that you can make a good profit on the property as well. You have to look at the different locations for the properties that you are considering. The type of person you would like to rent or sell the property to can matter as well. Families want quiet neighborhoods near schools and parks, while the elderly would like to be somewhere that is quiet and has other seniors who live there too. It all depends on the target audience you are going with.

What are the Steps to Use to Evaluate a Property Value?

Now it is time to do the evaluation on the property value to see what you are able to do with a property. Keep in mind that sometimes these steps will show you that a property is not going to work for your needs. Some of the things that you can do to help see whether the property is good for you or not include:

1. Determine the fair market value: This is the price that a buyer is willing to pay and that the seller is willing to take on the property. you can look at a few different tools to help with this like MLS comps, Zillow, the property appraisal and more.
2. Determine the replacement cost> This is going to be the amount of money it would take if you tried to construct the same property today. This can include the value of the land and the cost of materials and labor.
3. The market rent: If you plan to get this property and rent it out, you will want to take a look at the current rental rates and see if it is at market. If it is too high, the tenant may not want to renew the lease. If you have it below market, then you could have the potential to raise it or do some other things later on.

4. Determining the costs of updates: If you plan to update the property and flip it, then it is time for you to look at the current market value of the property, how much the repairs will cost, and what the market rate will be when all of the work is done. If you do the math and come out ahead, it could be a good option.

5. Calculate the NOI: This is the net operating income. This is found by subtracting the normal operating expenses from the gross income. This will include all the maintenance and repairs, the insurance, taxes, utilities, and the management fees on the property. this will not include the mortgage so factor that in as well.

6. Figure out how much it will cost until you can see: While your goal needs to be to get into the property as quickly as possible, you will need to take a few weeks at least to get it fixed up and then on the market. Then it can take a bit to sell and the closing time is not easy either. You need to plan on at least a few months of operating expenses, even if you plan to sell.

The investor needs to consider all aspects of this purchase. The goal is to make money, not live in the property, which means that things need to be handled in a different way than they would if you planned to live in the facility. Take some time to crunch the numbers and see whether a property is worth the investment or not.

Know When to Walk Away

One thing that an investor needs to do is know when to walk away. Sometimes this is at the beginning of the process. They may take a look at a property and then decide that it is too much work or that it costs too much for what they will be able to afford for that given property. When you go to look at a property, you must mentally prepare yourself for the fact that the property may be too high priced.

Do not fall into the trap of stretching your budget too much to make it work. This is really tempting to do, especially if the property is in a good area or you are excited to get started. You may want to stretch the numbers and say that it will all work out. But this can often eat into your profits and can make it hard if you pick out the wrong property.

Another thing to watch out for is a bidding war. Many sellers like to try to do this at an auction to see if they can get a higher price. In some auctions, you can get a good deal, but there is also the potential to get swept away in the excitement and then spend way more money than you wanted to in the first place, putting you in the home. If you go to a bidding war (though it is probably best to avoid for some time until you get more experience), have a number in place and do not go above it.

Even during regular negotiations, it is possible that the sellers will try to get more money from you to earn as much in profits as possible. You may offer less than the asking price to try and get a good deal. Have a good number in place as the maximum you are willing to stay, and then stick with it, being willing to walk away if the seller will not come down to the price that you want.

This is one of the hardest things to do in real estate investing. You may have your heart set on getting things done and purchasing a property. You need to look at this as a business and be careful with the money that you are spending. This means that you need to be willing to walk away when things are not matching up financially.

Having a good plan in place is the best way to make this happen. When you know ahead of time what you can afford and what you will be able to get out of the property, whether you flip it or use it as rental income, can make a difference. When. You can see on paper that the finances are not working out and that you will lose X amount of money in the process, it is much easier to see that the property is not a good one for you, which then makes it easier to walk away from the property.

Chapter 5: Financing Your Investment

Now it is time to look at the financing of things. Unless you have been saving up for a long time, it is not likely that you will have enough money to purchase a home, get the renovations done, and hold onto it until you get a tenant or sell it out of your own money. You will need some financing to get it all done. the good news is that there are a lot of great options that can help an investor get started. Let's take a look at some of the different ways that you can finance your investment of residential real estate.

Look at FHA Loans

If this is your first investment into real estate, you could consider getting a mortgage that is insured through the Federal Housing Administration. With just 3.5% down, you can pick out some of the options that work the best for you. this is a good option for getting a duplex option and living in one part while you rent out the other units and start investing. You will be able to live in the property rent free and make some money on it as well. This gets you into the investment and then you are able to see whether investing in this way is the right way for you.

Hard Money Loans

One of the main problems with a traditional mortgage is that they can take 60 days or more to close. If you are trying to make a deal quickly and want to get into investing without all of the waiting, then a hard money loan is one thing to consider. These are beneficial in that they have you a lot of flexibility to get to the property quickly and move up the closing date, but you need to be careful because the higher interest rates are higher.

Overall, this is not the best option to do long-term. But if you need to close on the property as fast as possible, it can work. For your first property, it can be a god way to gain some capital from the rental income or from the sale of the home, and then you can use other methods from there.

Non-Bank Mortgage Lending

For some types of real estate investing, you may find that it is hard to qualify for a traditional mortgage. There are other options out there to try. There are several types of non-bank lenders, like LendingHome and SoFI who are taking the market share away from some of the traditional banks.

Unlike some of the big banks out there, who will look at a lot of information about you, including tax returns, FICO score, and income, online lenders are able to process the application online in just 20 minutes. They can often get the work done within two weeks, rather than up to 60 days for a traditional bank. And it is possible to get the full purchase price of the home put into it as well, making it a good option for a lot of investors.

Cash Financing

For those who already have a lot of cash to help them get started, it is possible to do cash financing on the property. You would then be able to purchase the property clear and free, without having to worry about interest rates and more. This one is hard to do on your own because it requires a lot of money to even get started. But you can save up for a while or create a network of investors, friends, and family to help you have enough.

Private Money Lenders

If you are connected well, you could look at some of your personal connections to see whether this is a good option for you. Private money lenders are often going to be individuals or small companies who are willing to lend out money directly to the investor. There will be a specific interest rate and payback period that is discussed right at the beginning of the loan so there are no confusions. And if you know some of the private money lenders, you may increase your chances of getting the money that you need.

Self-Directed IRA Accounts

This one works the best if you have already started to do a plan through an IRA. You will need to work on this before you plan to purchase a property so that there is enough money to get it done. If you already have a self-directed IRA, you may be able to tap into the account to get some of the capital that you need to purchase the property. Just make sure to talk with your financial advisor to weigh the benefits and negatives of this to see if it is a good idea or not.

Seller Financing

There are a few times when the investor and the seller will be able to do something together known as seller financing. In this option, the property buyer is going to make payments right to the person selling the property, rather than having to deal with the bank at all. this is going to help a seller who is really motivated to sell the property faster. The investor will be able to avoid jumping over some of the traditional hurdles of lending, such as credit score minimums, and having to put a large amount of cash down.

With this option, the seller and the buyer will be able to enjoy a faster process of selling the home and can avoid many of the fees and costs associated with closing on the home. In addition, the owner can sell the promissory note if they do not want to manage the owner financing at a later time.

Peer to Peer Lending

Peer to peer lending is going to allow an investor to borrow money form other investors or a group of investors. The basic process is similar to hard or private money lending, though some of the specifics of this will be different. This can work for some investors because it allows them to bypass the traditional funding requirements and they can let the portfolio that they have do the work for them.

This form of real estate financing is often going to include a lower loan to value ratio compared to some of the other types. This will make it hard for the investor to borrow the entire amount of the loan to make the purchase. You may need to come up with more of the down payment to make this work. This peer to peer financing is going to offer a lot more flexibility to the work that you want to get done with investing, so it is a good option to choose.

What Loans are Good for Real Estate Investing?

When you are looking at all of your options for financing real estate, you need to take a look at a wide variety of different loans to see which one is going to work the best. Loans are some of the most common types of funding that a residential real estate investor will choose. These have the least amount of risks, often have the lower interest rates, and will work the best for paying things back when the investment is done. There are actually a good number of different loans that you will be able to choose from as a residential real estate investor and these include:

1. 203K loan: This is a loan that is backed by the FHA. They will help when the investor would like to purchase a property that is older or very damaged in order to fix them up.
2. Home equity loan: If a homeowner has built up some equity in their own personal home, they could take out a loan as a line of credit based on that equity. Allowing them this flexibility to expand their portfolios by using their home as the collateral.
3. FHA loan: For the consumer with less than perfect credit or those who do not have access to a lot of capital for a good down payment, homeownership is still a good option through the FHA program.
4. Traditional mortgage loan: Conventional home loans that are financed by banks is still a popular method for you to finance the real estate deal.
5. Conforming loans: This type of mortgage is going to be equal to or less than the amount that is established by the FHFA for a conforming loan limit. It is also going to match up with some of the requirements by Fannie Mae and Freddie Mac.
6. Portfolio Loan: These loans are going to be serviced through the initial lenders that issued the funds to start.

Instead of selling the loan to a secondary market, they will keep the loan in their own portfolio.

7. VA loans: If you qualify, it is possible to go for a VA loan through the United States Department of Veterans Affairs. This will only work for some borrowers who are able to qualify due to their VA status.

Each of these methods will have their own benefits and drawbacks that the investor will need to determine ahead of time. You may need to take some time to look at the options and compare them side by side to see which will provide you with the best results. Consider the length of the loan, the interest rate, and any fees that you will need to pay on the loan before getting started. This will help you be prepared when it comes to the investment and will help you to keep the costs as low as possible.

Now all loans will work for all investors. It can depend on the property you would like to invest in, the cash you have on hand, your location, and even your credit score. Working on your credit score ahead of time will make it easier to get some of the financing that you need too for these properties too. Since most investors are not going to have the money or cash upfront to do the purchase on their own, it is important that they know all of the financing options to help them start that investment.

How to Improve Chances of Getting Financing?

While there are many different types of financing that the residential real estate property can rely on, there are also a few steps that you can choose to help you increase your chances of getting some of that financing in the first place. A few steps that all investors should consider include:

- Choose the right lending type: An investor needs to do their research and then determine what type of lending is right for them. There are many types, but choosing the right one is going to help them get the most likelihood that they are going to get the funding. They may need to try out more than one type of funding to determine which one will help them the most.

- Work on your credit score: Investors who have poor credit scores will find that it is almost impossible for them to get some of the funding that they need. If you have some issues with your credit score already, then you need to take some time to improve the score. Even if the score is good, you need to look at ways to maintain that and raise it, making it easier for you to get some of the financing that you need.

- Have cash on hand: The more money that you will have on hand, the easier it is to get some of the money that you need for the investment. A larger down payment can go a long way in helping for your approval odds. And while it is not likely to happen, having the full amount for the investment property will make a big difference because you can purchase the property outright, without needing to worry about any type of financing in the first place.

- Try more than one lending option: You should consider doing more than one type of lender to make sure that you are getting the best deal. Going with the first person who offers you money may sound like a good way to get things done, but it is going to ruin you and make it harder for you to get a lower interest rate or better terms on the loan too. Talk to more than one lender and see if there are different types of financing that will work the best for you.

It is impossible to get the property that you want if you do not first work to get the right financing. With some of the steps above, you will be able to work on the financing part and get the best terms possible for the money you need for the new investment. Take the time to talk to as many people as possible and check out as many different forms of financing in order to help you out.

Chapter 6: Tax Implications of Real Estate Investing

When it is time to get into residential real estate, you need to make sure that you are prepared for everything. Part of this is the taxes that you will need to pay on the profits that you earn. While there are some rules in place that allow individuals to sell their property and purchase another one without having to pay the taxes on it, these rules are not going to apply to the investor who is trying to turn this into an income.

There are certain steps that you can take as a real estate investor to make sure that you can manage your tax bill at the end of the year while also maximizing the after tax return on the investment. Before we do that though, we need to take a closer look at some of the different ways that your properties will get taxed, making it easier to know how much your tax bill will be at the end of the year. Working with an accountant or a CPA is one of the best decisions that you can make to help keep the taxes in order.

Taxation of Rental Income

The first thing that we need to look at is the taxation of rental income. The IRS will be able to tax the real estate portfolios of investors in two ways. They can do this through capital gains tax and income tax. It is possible to also do an estate tax, but this is passed on after you are no longer alive.

Rental income is something that is taxable, just like ordinary income tax that you would pay for for working a regular job. That means that you need to declare it as income on the tax return and pay income tax on it. Unlike wages though, the income that you make on rental properties will not be subject to any of the FICA taxes though.

Your income here is going to be anything that you get from the rent or the royalties on the properties. You can then minus all of the deductible expenses. You will not be allowed to deduct everything through this as well. For example, you are only allowed to deduct mortgage interest and any repairs that you make to the property to make it functional again. You will not be able to do any capital investments like new buildings, big renovations, or additions to the property.

Capital Gains Taxes

There is also a second tax bill that an investor will need to focus on and this is known as the capital gains tax. The IRS is going to tax the investor on the net profits that they get from the property when they sell. If you plan to flip properties and you own it for less than a year, you will need to pay the short-term capital gains tax.

This is going to be the same rate as your marginal income tax and is based on how much you earn.

If you hold onto the property for 12 months or more, then you will qualify for the more favorable long-term capital gains, but then you have to pay the mortgage for that amount of time as well. This will be a smaller amount of tax compared to the short-term capital gains tax so it could be worth it for those who need more time working on the property.

You will need to pay capital gains tax on the difference between your selling price on the property and the adjusted tax basis. Your adjusted tax basis on the property will simply be the original cost that you paid for the property, along with the amount that you invest in improvements and renovations that were not deducted for taxes earlier.

If you have any deductions that are associated with the property, you will need to subtract them from the tax basis. If your adjusted tax basis is higher than the sale, then. You will end up with a capital loss. You will be able to subtract any capital losses from a given year from the capital gains to help reduce the tax bill.

It is also possible for the investor to take their capital losses and carry them forward into future years. This will help to keep your tax bill lower in the future when you start to earn more and have higher capital gains. If you have no capital gains, you can continue to deduct $3000 each year until all of your capital losses are carried forward.

Depreciation and Amortization

We also need to take a look at the depreciation and amortization of this process to help us out at tax time. This is a broad concept, but we can talk about some of the basics to help you get started. When you purchase a new property, whether it is a building or something else, the IRS knows that the item will get older as time goes on. This is going to make it decrease in value. Depreciation is going to be the process of claiming a deduction to compensate for the decrease in value of that property during the year.

Keep in mind that you are not able to depreciate your personal residence. You can only do this for an investment property. Land will also not depreciate, but the minerals that are under the land. If you plan to extract oil or other minerals, or even timber, from the land, you can use depletion to account for the gradual loss of value to that area.

When you purchase an investment real estate property and it has a useful life of longer than a year, the IRS knows that you will use that property to generate a long-term income. Outside of a few special circumstances, the IRS is not going to allow you to deduct the full amount of your investment in that first year. You will need to amortize the investment over a number of years. For real estate, this deduction is spread out over 27.5 years. You may not get the full deduction if you do not keep the property as long.

Passive Activity Rules

Investing in real estate can become a passive income stream if you work with a property manager and have other options in place. There are some complex rules that come with having passive real estate. If you are a passive investor though, it means that you are not doing the day to day work of managing your investment. This makes it so that you will need to follow the passive activity rules.

Basically, you are only going to be able to deduct the passive losses to the extend that you are able to cancel out the gains from passive activities. This is put in place to restrict your ability to use passive activity losses to offset some of the capital gains that you get in other parts of the portfolio. Most individual investor landlords are able to deduct a maximum of $25,000 a year in losses on their rental properties if necessary.

Property Taxes

When you own a residential property, you will need to pay property taxes. These go to the local and county government and you will need to pay them each year. Your local government is responsible for accessing the market value of the property at its highest and best use. And then they will take a percentage of that value each year in property taxes. You will be able to deduct these taxes against the rental income, as long as the property tax is uniformly assessed throughout the jurisdiction and is not a special assessment along the way.

Other Tax Deductions

When you get into the business of being a real estate investor, you will want to find as many tax deductions as possible. This helps you to keep more money in your own pocket and will make it easier for you to see results with your investment. There are several places where you can make deductions at tax time for your investment. Some of the most common will include

1. Interest you pay on the mortgage
2. Any legal fees that you pay that relate back to the investment property
3. Mileage to do the work with the property
4. Business use of the home through the home office deduction
5. Advertising fees

You may be able to deduct some of the costs of employees that you have to hire, but this one can be a little more difficult. You may need to work with a CPA to see whether you can deduct these expenses or if they need to be amortized for the best results.

Legal Entity Options for Your Real Estate Business

As you get more into being a real estate investor, there are a few types of business entities that you can choose to use. These all work differently and will depend on what you want to get done, how you plan to save on taxes and more. If you have a CPA working with you, they will be able to answer some questions on how to choose a legal entity. There are quire a few, and there is not really a wrong answer when it comes to which one to choose. It all depends on how you would like to run. Your business.

Some of the types of business entities that you can decide for your business includes:

Limited Liability Company or LLC

This is a good one for those who want to do rental property. they allow a mixture of pass-through taxation and limited liability protection. Your risk is going to be limited to the investment you make with the LLC. The IRS is often not going to tax the LLC itself, so there are no issues with double taxation.

The main claim to fame on this one is that it is more customizable. Unlike a corporation, which have a lot of rules to it, the LLC owner will have a lot of great flexibility. In the operating agreement with the LLC, the members will be able to craft their own rules for management, profit splitting, and adding in more people to the business. These are often easier to set up as well.

While the LLC is going to offer pass-through taxation, the income from the active businesses will have to go through the self-employment tax. You will not be able to pay yourself a salary or take dividends like you can with the S-corporation, which can make it harder to work with.

Overall, a LLC allows for limited liability so that the members will not be liable for the corporate debts and obligations, there is no double taxation, and you can even do fundraising if needed. If you plan to purchase properties to rent out to tenants, then the LLC entity may be one of the best for you.

S-Corporation

For those who would like to flip homes, the S-corporation is a good one to choose. One tax benefit is that it provides pass-through taxation. That is just the start to the tax benefits of working with this one. Individuals who do active business, such as flipping homes, will have to pay self-employment tax on the income. This is not going to happen if you have a rental income that is passive instead. The current self-employment tax rate is at 15.3%.

When you use an S-corporation, as long as you provide yourself with a reasonable salary, you can take the rest of the profits through dividends, which will not go through the self-employment tax. You will have to pay this tax on your own salary, but not on the rest, which is going to save you a lot of money.

The liability is nice on this one because you will not be liable for the corporate debts and there is no double taxation. After paying the reasonable salary, the owners will take the rest of the income as dividends, which will not need to go through the self-employment tax. The administration part of this is often the hardest because there need to be formation documents, corporate minutes, and periodic government filings.

Sole Proprietorships

Most real estate investors are going to start out as a sole proprietorship. These allow you to do the work on your own and you do not form any legal entity at all. This is not really a legal entity at all and is not going to provide a lot of protection to you if something goes wrong. But just by starting the investment, you are already a sole proprietorship, with no paperwork or other things to get done.

While the sole proprietorship is not going to require filing fees or a lot of legal documents, those who go with this option will have unlimited liability for the debts and the obligations on the business. this means that if someone gets injured while living in the property or you have an issue with a contractor getting hurt doing a job, they will be able to go after all of your personal assets.

General Partnerships

This one is similar to the sole proprietorship, but there will be more than one person working together to get the investment started. There are no filing fees, no legal documents, and nothing else that you need to do. Each partner in that general partnership will be liable for any obligations of the partnership, even the liabilities that some of the other partners incur. This means that you need to really trust the people you work with in this method.

The advantages of this is that you will only be taxed once on the earnings. And the administration is simple because there are no formation documents, government reports, or filing fees. The liability is higher than the others though and you could be on the hook for a lot of money if you are not careful with this option.

Each of these entities can be a good one for you to choose, but you need to research and figure out which one will be right for how you want to run your business. Talk to a CPA to see whether one or the other of these legal business entities make the most sense for how you wish to run your business.

Working with a CPA

Unless you have experience in accounting and a lot of time on your hands to learn about the different tax breaks and tax implications of your real estate investment, it may be a good idea to work with a CPA to help handle all of the financial aspects. The CPA may cost a bit upfront, but they are worth it and can save you thousands of dollars each year as your empire grows.

CPAs know how to handle all of the financial parts of your business. They can gather the documents, look for deductions, and keep your tax bill as low as possible. They will even take a look at some of the ways that you run your business and can give suggestions on ways that you can make improvements and see more profits.

It is likely that the CPA is better at taxes and money than you are. This means that it is worth your time to be nice to them and have one on your team. They can take care of some of the pesky paperwork while you focus on getting the property ready to go to make more money in the process.

Chapter 7: Do I Need a Property Manager?

One question that you may need to ask is whether it is a good idea to have a property manager help you take care of your properties. The property manager is someone who is responsible for your property, who will take care of tenant complaints, fix up the properties, clean them out when a tenant leaves, and can help you advertise and vet new tenants.

If you just have one or two rental properties, it is likely that you can do all of the work on your own. As your empire grows, you may find that it takes a lot of time to be a landlord and this can be hard to do on your own. Or maybe you want to turn this into a passive income and would like to have someone else take over some of the work. This is what a property manager can do for you.

To pay the property manager, you will need to give them a percentage of your rental income. This can often be between 10 to 15% of the total rental income. This can be negotiated depending on the properties that you would like to work with too. Not all landlords will need a property manager, but some of the things that you can consider when choosing whether to get a property manager or not includes:

Is the Rental Property Close to Home?

The first thing to consider when you want to hire a property manager or do the work yourself is how far the rental property is to your current location or home. The more miles that you have between you and the investment property, the harder it is going to be for you to manage that property. if your primary residence is in Illinois and the rental property is in Florida, it is harder to be a landlord.

Even with the distance, you will still need to find tenants to occupy the property, handle any complaints that come up, respond to emergencies that happen quickly, and even make sure that the rent is collected on time. If you live across the country, it is really hard to get this done. You may need to take the time to hire on a property manager who is closer to the property to do the work for you.

The time it takes for the investor to get to the property and the cost of getting there can add up quickly. In situations where you can't be there to be a good landlord, but you still want to make a good income in the process, it is a good idea to hire a property manager. In the long run, this property manager is going to help you to save money and see your profits grow.

How Many Units Will You Own?

While an investor may be able to handle the property management of one or two properties, the more units they own, the harder this becomes. There are more responsibilities the more units that you own. And with more tenants, you have more issues, maintenance, complaints, and even vacancies to deal with. If you can't devote all of your time to this, then it may be time to hire a property manager.

IN addition, if you have a lot of units and they are spread out between different properties or even different towns, you are going to need to give up more of your time to manage the cash flow of each property while also commuting from each property to help handle the issues that show up. A property manager will be able to take over this for you, making sure that you can handle all of your units, no matter how many you have.

Do You Have Experience Managing Property?

If your goal is to invest in real estate, but you really know nothing about managing the property, then hiring a good property manager is going to be one of the best choices that you can make. Learning as you go in this market is going to be expensive and it can be worth it to find someone else to do some of the work for you.

For a property investor who is just getting started, taking too long to fill up one of the vacancies in the building or hiring the wrong professional to repair something can eat into your income. Mistakes such as being accused of discrimination because you were unfamiliar with Fair Housing laws or of being called a slum lord because the heat was not fixed fast enough, can be enough to ruin all of your hard work in this investment.

Along the same lines, you need to be careful about the type of property manager you would like to hire. Hiring one who is not good at their job can destroy your investment. This is why you should do some research and screen any property manager you are considering before you choose the one that is right for you.

Can You Afford the Property Manager?

Another thing to consider is whether you are able to afford the property manager. You have to have a good handle on your finances. You will need to pay the property manager. Most will charge around 10% for the work that they do. If you have ten or more properties, it is possible to get the amount down, but you will need to talk to several property managers to see what price you are given.

You will need to figure out how much rent you are able to charge for the property and then figure out the fee that the property manager would like to charge. The higher the percentage, the more it is going to cost you out of the rent. Finding a good property manager who provides their services for a good rate will be important here. This can help you get the services that you need without all of the costs.

Always look at some of the extra fees that the property manager is going to charge too. It is common for some to charge tenant placement fees, which is simply their bonus for helping you find the tenant you would like to use in your properties. These fees can vary based on what the property manager would like to charge. You will need to talk to the property manager to see what will want to charge and see if it works for your budget and finances on the rental property.

Do You Have Time to Manage the Property?

Sometimes the investor is not going to have the necessary time to manager their own properties. If you own a couple rental properties and have a full-time job at the same time, you may find that your hours are limited and you are not able to get over to that property. Your property needs attention and help to thrive well. Otherwise, it is not going to be successful and you may have to sell them and give up. A property manager can take over while you do some of the other work you need to get done.

You also need to realize that time is money and managing a property is something that takes time. If you feel that all of the obligations that come with managing your property will take away from time that you could spend making money at another job or investing in more properties, then it is a good idea to hire a property manager to help out instead.

Are You Willing to Give Up Control?

When you hire a property manager, you will get a chance to let someone else take control and handle your property for you. for some investors, this is the welcome break that they need, allowing them to focus on their investment or finding more properties to add to their portfolio. But for others, giving up this control is not an easy task.

Property managers will be in charge of everything from collecting rent from your tenants to filing taxes for the property. As the investor, you need to be willing to give the property manager that much control. While the property manager may have experience and a certification, you have to consider whether they have the same passion for the investment as you, and whether you are willing to give up some of that control over the property to the property manager.

What is Your Tolerance for Dealing with Tenants?

Dealing with tenants is something that takes a special person to get done. It is not always easy and you may not always get the good tenants that you want. If you are worried about finding tenants, dealing with evictions, or any other problems with the tenant, then it is time to look at a property management.

If the stress of dealing with tenants will take a toll on you, then it is time to work with a property manager. These professionals are skilled at handling all of the potential landlord-tenant conflict. They understand how landlord-tenant laws work and can work as a buffer for most of the problems that will arise. And when the tenant knows that they are dealing with the property manager, they may also act more professional in the process.

Deciding to work with a property manager is a personal experience. It will take some of the profits out of your rental income, but for many landlords, the cost is worth it. This is a good way to limit the work that you have to do, making the rental property more of a passive income, while allowing you to still have the properties as your own and giving you more time to look for new properties later.

Chapter 8: Using Contractors or Doing the Work Yourself?

As a real estate investor, you need to make some good decisions to ensure that you make as much money as possible. Whether you are flipping a home or trying to get it ready for some tenants to move in, you may need to do a bit of work on the property to get it up to code and make it look nice.

Most of the time, doing the work yourself will save the most money. You will not need to pay for the time and labor of the contractor, which can save you a lot along the way. However, this does take a lot longer to get the work done. You will also not be able to buy the items at discount or in bulk like a contractor can do, which will drive some of the costs of the project up more than the costs of the contractor.

Many investors will do a combination. They will bring in a contractor to help with some of the work, like foundation work or handling some of the issues with electricity. Then they will take on some of the smaller work, like changing the floors or doing some painting. You will need to talk to several contractors for the work that you want done, usually during the closing process so they can get into the home right away after closing, and get some quotes to see how much things will cost you.

With a cost analysis, you can determine whether it makes the most sense to hire someone to get the work done right and quickly, preventing problems and getting the property ready for you to sell or rent out to someone else. You can then take on the rest of the work at the same time so that it gets done quickly and you are able to make as much money on the property as possible.

When Should I Pay a Contractor?

While you may be able to save some money doing the work on your own for real estate, you may find that it is a better idea to work with a contractor to do some of the work. A few cases where you should consider hiring a contractor to help get the work done in your residential real estate property includes:

The Work Isn't Safe

There may be some projects that need to be done around the property to make it livable, but it is not safe for you to do the work on your own. It is one thing to take on some unpleasant renovation work like repainting the deck or doing some re-grouting in the bathroom tiles. But if there is the potential that the project is going to be dangerous, then it is a good idea for you to hire a professional contractor to do the work.

Some examples of some work that is not all that safe for most people to do on their own will include:

1. Electrical work. Unless you have training as an electrician, it is generally best to not try to do this on your own.
2. Landscaping that is going to require a lot of heavy lifting or specialized machinery to get it all done.
3. Roofing projects, no matter what size they are.

You should always be on the safe side. While it would be nice to have things cost less because you do it on your own, if you end up injuring yourself, it can cost more in medical bills and will take the project more time to get a tenant in or to do a flip of the home. For most investors, it is better to hire a professional to do the work rather than taking on the risk.

The Work is Complicated

Sometimes the work is too complicated or it will need a professional to do it to keep it up to code. Some projects that you want to do, like painting and changing the carpet, are fine for a beginner to do. But there are some big projects that even someone with advanced skills may struggle to do. This will usually revolve around the electricity and the plumbing that you want to do in the home.

For example, you may think that it is a good idea to do the water heater on your own. But what happens if you break one of the pipes while you are doing the work? This is going to cause a major leak and you will need to spend money on an emergency now. If there is work that needs to be done on the electrical components of the home, you will need to bring in the professionals to keep it up to code.

The Work Takes Too Much Time

Depending on the experience that you have with your own home renovations, you may be able to do some of the projects that you need without needing to hire a contractor. But if you are looking at some work that will need a lot of hours of labor, it may be a good idea for you to hire a contractor rather than taking the time around your busy schedule and hoping that it does not drag on for too long.

Imagine that you have a home where the basement needs to get done. You may have some of the skills to put up the walls, do some work on the flooring and painting, but it does take a long time. You may take the time when you are doing it in your own home, but you need it done quickly when it comes to an investment. This may make it a good option to hire a contractor to help you get it done.

While it could take you six months to get a project done around your already busy schedule, a contractor is a professional who can do it in less time. They may be able to get it done in four weeks instead. This can speed up the process so that you can flip the home faster or turn it into a rental income rather than holding it empty for a long time either.

You Don't Have Time

Some of the home renovations that you want to do are going to be simple, but they are going to require a good deal of patience and time as well. For example, installing a backsplash in your kitchen is simple enough to do, but it is going to take forever. But if you would have to take off work to do it, and you make a good amount at work, it may be worth your time to hire a contractor to do some of the home improvement projects while you continue to work and do other things with your time.

Let's say that the time you would need to spend on a project would cost you $150 for the contractor to get the work done. But if you are able to make $200 in that same time period doing your regular job or freelancing, it may be a good idea to just hire the contractor to get it done. It is your investment, but you will need to balance out the costs of your investment and see whether it is worth your time to do the work or if you should hire another contractor to do it.

Your residential real estate property is going to need to get some work done. That is how you got it for such a good price. You will need to balance out the benefits and negatives to figure out whether it is worth your time to do the work yourself or hire a contractor to do it. For some things, like electricity and plumbing in the home, you have no choice but to call in the professionals to keep the home up to code. But for some other projects, you will have some freedom in the work that you can do and whether you hire someone or do the work yourself.

Chapter 9: Potential Barriers and Fears

There are a lot of benefits that come with residential real estate investing. You are excited to get started in this new investment form investing, whether you want to become a landlord or you are looking to flip a home and make a profit. However, there are large sums of money that are exchanged in all real estate transactions and risking that much money can be scary to many people who first jump in. Some of the potential barriers and fears that residential real estate investors will feel include:

I Will Fail

This is a normal feeling that many new investors are worried about. They do not want to waste their money on a bad investment and since this involves a lot of money to get things done, they are nervous to get things done. You will need to work on your mindset to help you overcome this fear and to make sure that you are prepared to take on this big investment to see results along the way.

There are different ways that you can prepare. You can read books about being successful in real estate and seeing yourself meet your goals. You can study the market to see what things are selling for and how much you can earn on potential deals. You can save up money to make it easier to get the funding in place. And you can craft a good plan to help you along the way. When all of these components come together, it is much easier for you to be successful, rather than fail, at real estate investing.

I Can't Invest Long Distance

Sometimes the best deals in real estate are going to be far away from home. And this can make some first-time investors a little bit nervous. They may wonder how they will be able to invest in something that they are not able to see before they get there. This can cause many of them to choose to only invest in residential properties that are near their home, rather than venturing out to other locations.

Thinking this way is smart because it ensures that you do not jump right into a property that is bad for you. Ending your research right there though will make you miss out on a lot of potential properties that are good for you. Instead of just writing off a property because the distance is a little further away, it is a good idea for you to consider having an inspector look over the property.

The inspector will be able to provide a good analysis of the property, which often has a written report with pictures, and can list out some of the items that they would recommend. This can help you to see whether there are a lot of issues. You can then make a decision on whether this property is a good one for you to invest in or not.

I Should Use My Money for Something Else

While the idea of making a lot of money in real estate can be appealing, many worry that they are just going to throw money down the drain and not get ahead. They may wonder why they should choose to invest in real estate when they could buy stocks through a brokerage. While this kind of investment can be easier and sometimes provide more peace of mind, it is not as lucrative or as much fun as investing in real estate.

When you are doing an investment, you must remember there will be an opportunity cost for everything that you do. While there is some risk with this type of investment, there is a lot of reward as well. You can easily turn this into a passive income, which is hard to do with the stock market. And rentals are a good option, no matter how the economy is going.

Think of how many ways that you can make money in real estate. You can purchase and flip a home. You can purchase a home and then live in part of it and rent out the rest. You could become a landlord and earn rental income for a number of years and then sell the property, earning on the updates and the appreciation on the property. there are very few investments that provide the same kind of opportunities as real estate, which makes it a good option to choose.

Scaling Real Estate is Hard

Some beginners are going to be worried that scaling their real estate business will be too hard. With scaling in real estate, we are often talking about having enough capital to help purchase a property quickly and enough cash flow each month to have the freedom that you want. This is a big dream and goal of residential real estate investing, but scaling to that level will take some time and commitment.

Scaling does take some time to do, but it is possible to do. You will need to start out small and pick out the right properties. As you go through one property after another, you will be able to scale your real estate business and be one of the big investors out there with your own real estate empire.

Experienced Investors Will Find Better Deals

As a new investor, you may assume that you stand no chance against some of the more experienced investors who are out there. They have been in the market a long time, have their system down, and have more money at their disposal. This can be true, but that does not mean that all hope is lost. For example, since the experienced investor has their own system down, it is likely that they will pass up on some perfectly good residential real estate investments because they do not fit the right mold, not because they are bad investments.

There are always going to be those investors who will have a better deal flow, more experience, more contacts, and more capital to spend on the real estate. This is just something that you need to acknowledge and work through. With more experience, you will gain more confidence to make it through with the investment. You will get your own system in place and see better results as time goes on too.

I Will Make a Bad Decision

One of the biggest fears that a new real estate investor will have is that they will make a bad choice with their investment and choose a bad property. if you go through some of the steps above and really do an analysis of the market before jumping in, you will never make a bad decision in real estate. You will learn how to walk away from a bad property and focus only on the ones that are a good investment.

Keep in mind that no matter how much work you put into it, you have to dive in at some point. And that first property is likely not to be a slam dunk. You will learn as you go a bit in this industry and there will be mistakes that are made. However, when you have the long-term view, these mistakes can become chances for you to learn and you can take that knowledge over to the next deal that you want to do.

Things are going to go wrong with a property that you have. That is just part of the investment. But the important thing here is to remember that you are learning and that you take those mistakes and turn them into learning experiences. When you can do that, it is much easier for you to make good money in real estate.

I Will Not Be Able to Get Funding

Funding is often going to be one of the hardest parts of this kind of investment. You need to be ready to jump into this and take some of the rejections that will show up. It would be nice if the first bank offered you the money that you want with no problem, but this is not always the case. You may need to shop around a little bit to find the best deal.

We discussed many of the different financing options available to you in an earlier chapter. This is to show you that you do have options. If the traditional mortgage method does not work, that does not mean that all of your hopes and dreams are gone. It simply means that you move on to the next one.

Investors in residential real estate are going to shop around and find a lot of good options until they find the one that is right for them. This does take time and may require some rejection along the way. Prepare yourself for that as soon as possible and you can save a lot of heartache too. With the right perseverance, you will be able to find the funding that you need for your real estate investment in no time.

Learning to recognize some of the potential fears and issues that are going to show up in the real estate investing world is important. That is the best way to make sure that you will not end up with a mess along the way and you can be prepared to handle these issues. Every real estate investor is going to have some doubts and run into roadblocks as they go through this process. But it is about how they handle all of that which will determine whether they see their investment grow or not.

Chapter 10: Growing Your Real Estate Empire

Once you get done with your first property, you will be able to learn a lot. This is a good way to get yourself into the market and learn a lot. You are likely to make a lot of mistakes and have to ask for help at some point or another. And that s fine. As long as you are willing to learn along the way, you will be able to get ahead and do better on your next property.

The overall goal of getting into real estate is to create a real estate empire. This is going to help you to really earn the full income that you want and is the only way to turn all of this into a passive income. But many investors worry about how they will take that one property they start with and turn it into a second, third, and so on property for them to make money.

When you are ready to take your knowledge and turn it into a great empire that produces income, there are a few steps that you can take in to help with it. Some of these steps include:

Be Educated in How to Start

The best thing that you can do to help your investment succeed is to educate yourself on the market and how real estate works. You should not just hear one person talk about how great real estate investing is and then jump right in. This is the fastest way for you to fail in your goals when it comes to investing and it can be a lot of money to lose in the process.

Educating yourself before you jump into the investment is much smarter. Try to learn as much about residential real estate as possible. This can be a lot of fun and will prepare you for all of the challenges that may happen along the way.

A good place to start with reading. Find as many books about real estate that you can and learn about it. Learn how to find financing, how to find the best properties, and the different strategies that you are able to use for investing in this type of real estate. You will be able to look at books if you have a specific method of investing that you would like to use as well to ensure that you understand how it works.

That is just the start of what you will want to do when it comes to your residential real estate empire. You can listen to podcasts from others in the market, meet experts and follow their blogs, and look online to learn as much as possible. Look at the real estate market from many different angles to find the one that will work the best for you.

You should also take some time to investigate your own local market. What do homes typically go for in your area? Are there are lot of rentals and what are the prices for landlords who rent those out? What are the current interest rates and how is that going to affect the price that you pay for your property and what others will pay as well? You need to be very familiar with the market in your area, or the area you wish to invest in, before you even get started in this market.

Basically, the more time that you can take to learn about real estate and how it works, the better. This will help you be prepared for every part of the process and can avoid some of the big issues that can bother new investors when they get started in real estate. Get educated on how to handle real estate, take your time, and have the right funding to make all of this happen for your investment.

Set Clear Goals

The next thing that you need to consider is setting clear goals that you would like to accomplish along the way. There are a lot of different reasons to get into real estate, but if you do not have the clear goals that you would like. All investors will need to spend some time thinking through their goals to help you stay on track and do well in investing.

Before you jump into this process, take some time to set the clear goals that you need. These clear goals will direct you to the types of investments that you need to go for, the amount of risk that you are willing to take, and more. You should not follow the goals that someone else is doing. Take the time to come up with your own goals and your business in real estate will be more successful than before.

Keep Track of Your Finances

You need to put your finances to work with you. If you sell a home and then waste it all on something fun or you do not use your money smartly from the monthly rent, you will never have enough to purchase another property and start the process again. And that is the overall goal for all residential real estate investors out there.

You need to keep back some of the money from each property so that you are able to get properties in the future. You can use some of the money to help pay your own bills or for other needs, but at least a bit of it needs to be set aside for future investments. This will make it easier to purchase the property that you would like when another one becomes available. Do this for a few properties and you will start to see your empire grow.

If you are uncertain about how much to save back or you are worried about handling some of the financial aspects in a way that will help your business to grow, then it is time to talk to the CPA. They will be able to take a look at everything and will give you some of the advice that you need along the way. They can tell you when it is time to cut some costs, where you can invest the money, and how to make all of this work for your taxes too, making them a good asset to keep around.

Have an Investment Strategy

Never go into this type of investment without having a good strategy in place. This is important no matter what type of investment you would like to go with. You need to think about what type of investing you would like to do with your real estate money and then jump in from there. You can expand and do more than one strategy later as you build up, but for now you should just work with one type of strategy for the best results.

There are a lot of different investment strategies that you can try out for your needs. For example, if you plan to purchase and flip a home to make money, that is going to be one type of investment strategy for you to use. Or if you plan to purchase a lot of properties and rent them out to others, then this is another type of investment strategy that you are able to go with. You have so many different options available when it comes to the real estate market, but you need to pick one and stick with it for the best results.

You will find that investing in real estate is a big thing and shouldn't be taken lightly. If you go in without a plan or strategy in place or you do not think things through and want to dabble in more than one strategy at the same time, then you will fail. That is just the nature of the game. Take the time to research each of the options (we provide a chapter to help you learn more about all of them), and then pick one that aligns with your goals with real estate investing.

Get the First Property

The first step in investing in residential real estate is to purchase that first property. This can sometimes take a bit longer than an investor is used to. You may even put offers in on more than one property and have them turned down or have someone else outbid you for that property. That is just part of the process.

You need to stick with that in order to bring in that first property and see some of the results that you want. You will get that first property if you are willing to stick with it and you do not give in to the pressure to just grab a property, even if it does not fit in with some of your goals for real estate investing. It is much better to wait for the perfect property rather than jumping in with a property that is not going to be right for your needs.

Have Your Team Ready

As a beginner, you may do some of the work on the property on your own. But you can turn this into a truly passive income if you have your own crew to help you get it done. This will make sure that you are able to get the work done quickly so that you can bring tenants in or you can flip the home in no time.

There are a lot of people that you can add into your team based on what you want to do yourself and what you would like to hire someone else to do. You may need to have a real estate agent who will help you know the market and when there are new properties that will come on the market, making you more effective. They can even help point potential tenants your way when the property is done.

You should consider having contractors that can get the work done quickly for you. A general contractor is a good idea here because they can do a lot of the work on their own. Knowing a few can be a good idea in case the original is not able to get the work done on your timeline along the way. You can also hire an electrician and a plumber in case there is a good deal of work that needs to get done in the property as well.

From there, you can consider a property manager. The property manager is going to be a good option as you try to grow your empire more. You may not want to deal with all of the tenants or the day to day operations of your rental properties and hiring a property manager can help you out with that as well.

Having this team on hand is going to make life easier as you get more properties. They can be on-call so when the property is purchased, they can get to work quickly and you can start to make some more money along the way. This team can make your life a little bit easier and prevents you having to do all of the work yourself.

Buy More Properties

When you first start out with residential real estate, you will purchase one property. This is easy for you to manage and will help you to get your feet wet in this kind of investment. You may stick with one property at a time in the beginning. As you get more comfortable in real estate investing, you may find that it is time to branch out and purchase more properties and hold onto some of them.

Even if you start this out with flipping properties, you may get to the point where you will purchase several at a time to work on and flip, keeping yourself busy and having something in the works all of the time. This may take some time to get down, but will help you to earn more money and grow your own portfolio as well.

Diversify the Portfolio

As you get better at working through the process, the goal is to diversify some of your portfolio. This is important for any type of investment. The more diversity in the portfolio, the more money you can make with the least amount of the risk. In the beginning, you may only be able to work with one type of property and even just one property. This is a big investment and may be the only way that you will be able to afford to get started.

But, as you learn more about the real estate market and how it works and you explore some of the different components that come together, it is time to branch out. Maybe you started with just rental properties and now you add in some duplexes or you start flipping homes. You can even start to look more at some commercial properties to see if this is a way to make some money too. The overall goal is to add some diversity into the work that you do in the real estate market, honing your skills, making more money, and reducing the amount of risk that you take on when investing.

Growing a real estate business is not always as simple as it seems. You need to be willing to work hard and try out a few things to find your niche and turn this into a reality. And it is often much harder than it appears on your favorite television show. But as you start to work through this method of making money, you will find that it can start with one and quickly grow into having lots of properties and making a good income for you.

Conclusion

There are a lot of different types of investments that you may want to consider for your own needs. Picking the right one will make all the difference and can help you put your money to work for you. And real estate has a lot of applications, allowing you simple ways to make money the way that makes the most sense for you.

Whether you are looking to move into becoming a landlord, commercial real estate, or even fix and flips, you will find there are so many options for real estate. And it is possible to slowly grow your portfolio and see some amazing results. The hope of this guidebook is to help make that a reality for you!

If you have found this book helpful, please leave a review on Amazon! And when. You want to learn more about how to get rich and invest your money, check out the other books in our Get Filthy Rich series today!